PLANT CLONES

TEXT BY ELAINE PASCOE

PHOTOGRAPHS BY DWIGHT KUHN

BLACKBIRCH®
PRESS

THOMSON

GALE

San Diego • Detroit • New York • San Francisco • Cleveland • New Haven, Conn. • Waterville, Maine • London • Munich

THOMSON

GALE

For more information, contact
The Gale Group, Inc.
27500 Drake Rd.
Farmington Hills, MI 48331-3535
Or you can visit our Internet site at http://www.gale.com

Photo Credits: All pages © Dwight R. Kuhn Photography

LIBRARY OF CONGRESS CATALOGING-IN-PUBLICATION DATA

Pascoe, Elaine.
 Plant clones / by Elaine Pascoe.
    p. cm. — (Nature close up)
Summary: Describes plants that reproduce by creating perfect copies of themselves, how different plant parts generate these clones, and what a grower can do to encourage plant clones. Includes activites and experiments related to plants.
Includes bibliographical references and index.
 ISBN 1-56711-444-X (hardcover : alk. paper)
 1. Plants—Reproduction—Juvenile literature. 2. Clones (Plants)—Juvenile literature.
[1. Plants—Reproduction. 2. Clones (Plants) 3. Reproduction, Asexual. 4. Plants—Experiments. 5. Experiments.] I. Title II. Series: Pascoe, Elaine. Nature close-up.

QK826.P35 2003
575.4'9—dc21   2003011043

Printed in China
10 9 8 7 6 5 4 3 2 1

Contents

✼ ✼ ✼

1

Green Clones

Green clones blanket Earth!

It sounds like something from a science fiction movie. Yet there are green clones on Earth. Many plants make clones—perfect copies of themselves—all the time.

In fact, some of the plants you know best produce clones. Fruits and vegetables —such as strawberries, raspberries, onions, and potatoes can reproduce this way. Garden flowers—such as daffodils and irises make clones. So do many wild plants.

The ways in which plants clone themselves are amazing, but they are not just stunts. Producing offspring in these ways helps many types of plants survive.

Seeds or Not

Plants can reproduce in two very different ways. Flowering plants produce offspring by making seeds. Seeds form when male pollen reaches female egg cells in the heart of a flower. This is called sexual reproduction because it involves two sexes, male and female.

Right: The iris can reproduce in two ways— by making seeds and by making clones.

Below: Duckweed, a water plant, reproduces by making clones.

5

In many cases, pollen from one plant, carried by wind or bees or in some other way, reaches eggs of another plant. The seeds that form, and the plants that grow from them, have two parents. They get half their genes from each parent. Genes control the traits of the new plants, so the new plants combine traits from both parents. They are like their parents, but not exactly the same.

Many plants, including many flowering plants, can also reproduce without making male or female cells. The plant simply grows new "daughter" plants from its roots, stems, or leaves. This is called asexual, or vegetative, reproduction. A new plant that grows in this way has only one parent. It gets all its genes from that parent, so it has all the same traits. It's a clone.

Flowering plants reproduce by making seeds.

Tulips and daffodils are plants that produce both seeds and clones.

Above: A strawberry plant's seeds are carried on its berries.

Right: New strawberry plants grow from runners.

Lots of plants use both methods. Strawberry plants produce flowers and seeds, which are contained in their berries. If the seeds are planted, new plants will grow. But strawberry plants also send out runners—horizontal stems that grow out from the plant along the soil. The runners send new roots down into the soil, and new plants grow up from them.

Each method has advantages for the plants. Vegetative reproduction is a very good way for a plant to produce large numbers of offspring quickly. For strawberry plants, sending out runners uses less energy than making flowers, fruit, and seeds. The daughter plants that grow from runners are tougher than delicate seedlings, and they mature faster. And if the parent plant is well suited to its spot, its clones have a good chance of growing well alongside it.

But if too many daughter plants grow, they may become too crowded. Then none of the plants will do well. Seeds scatter widely, so they help plants spread to new areas. And because they combine traits of different parents, plants that grow from seeds help ensure variety within a species. If disease strikes or the climate changes, some of the plants may be better able to survive than others.

Plants can make new plants from stems, leaves, or roots. Different plants use different methods.

A dandelion's seeds are spread far and wide by the wind.

9

Plants from Stems

A thicket of black raspberry or blackberry bushes is really an army of clones. These plants can produce new plants from any stem. Their arching branches droop down to the ground. Along the branches are nodes—places from which new stems, leaves, or roots can grow. Wherever a node on the branch touches the soil, roots begin to grow and daughter shoots spring up. English ivy also spreads this way. Wherever its stems contact soil, ivy takes root and grows.

Blackberries are among the plants that produce clones from stems.

The runners that strawberry plants send out along the surface of the ground are really specialized stems. If you follow a runner to its tip, you will find a node. First the node produces a small rosette of leaves, the start of a daughter plant. As the daughter plant grows bigger, it produces its own root system. In time the runner dies, and the new plant is independent. Other plants that produce clones through runners include the spider plant, a popular houseplant.

A node at the tip of a strawberry runner gives rise to new roots and shoots.

Above: Ferns spread with the help of underground stems called rhizomes.

Right: Iris rhizomes look like roots, but they produce new plants.

Other plants produce clones from special stems that are hidden underground. Rhizomes are stems that grow horizontally below the soil. They look like roots, but they have buds that can send up new shoots. Those shoots develop into daughter plants. Iris and ferns spread by rhizomes. So do some grasses, including some that gardeners consider weeds. Their spreading rhizomes make these grasses hard to weed out!

Left: A potato tuber is the swollen tip of the potato plant's rhizome.

Above: New plants grow from the "eyes" of a potato.

A potato may not look like a stem, but it is. Potatoes are tubers—the swollen tips of rhizomes. Their "eyes" are buds that can grow into new shoots. The rest of the tuber contains stored food that helps the shoots grow while they develop new roots. One potato plant may produce many tubers, and each tuber can produce one or more new plants. Usually, the bud at the tip of the tuber sprouts first and gives rise to a new plant. But if that bud is damaged, other buds will sprout. And if a tuber is cut up, any piece with at least one bud can give rise to a daughter plant.

13

Shoots grow up from the tips of onion bulbs, and roots grow down from the base.

Onions, tulips, and daffodils grow from bulbs, another kind of underground stem. Bulbs are squat and round. The stem is shortened down to a disc, with thick, fleshy leaves that store food packed tightly above it. Roots grow down from the base of the bulb, and shoots grow up from the tip. Meanwhile, underground, new bulblets grow at the sides of the base. In time, they produce their own shoots and roots. In this way a single daffodil can grow into a big clump of flowers.

Corms look like bulbs and produce new plants in the same way. Inside, they are different because their food is stored in stem tissue, not in leaf tissue. Gladioli, crocuses, and freesias are corms. Corms send out side shoots that form small corms. Like bulblets, they can be separated and planted individually.

Daffodils also grow from bulbs. By making clones, a single bulb can become a clump of daffodils.

15

Plants From Roots and Leaves

Plant roots draw food and water from the soil and provide support for the plant. Plants such as radishes, carrots, and white sweet potatoes have fat roots that store food for the growing plant. And sometimes roots also help a plant reproduce.

The roots of red raspberries, aspens, and many other shrubs and trees send up root sprouts, or suckers, near the base of the parent plant. As the sprouts grow up, a single shrub can become a thicket. A single quaking aspen tree can become a grove.

Although this maple tree was cut down, new shoots are growing up from the roots.

Common milkweed is another plant that spreads by sending up new shoots from its roots. Since the root system of a milkweed plant can grow up to 10 feet (3 meters) a year, a patch of milkweed expands quickly.

Milkweed roots grow out from the plant and produce new shoots. In time the plants form a dense patch.

Tiny new plants form along the edge of a kalanchoe leaf.

In some plants, clones form from leaves. Two popular houseplants, kalanchoe and bryophyllum (also known as "mother of thousands" or the piggyback plant), produce new plants this way. Tiny buds form along the edges of the leaves. The buds develop into miniature plants, with their own tiny leaves and roots. These daughter plants break off, fall to the ground, and take root. Some water plants, such as duckweed, also reproduce this way.

Leaves of African violets, begonias, and some other plants can give rise to new plants, but in a different way. If you cut a leaf from one of these plants and keep the cut end in water or damp soil, it will eventually grow new roots and shoots. This is one of the ways in which people take advantage of plants' amazing ability to clone themselves.

African violet leaves will produce new plants if their stems are kept in damp soil.

19

Gardeners take advantage of plants' ability to make clones, with beautiful results.

Clones in the Garden

Home gardeners and commercial growers often use vegetative propagation to grow new plants. There are four main methods: division, layering, cutting, and grafting.

Division works well for plants that grow in clumps, with lots of short stems rising out of the ground. Hostas, daylilies, and irises are in this group. A gardener just needs to dig up the clump, split it apart roots and all, and replant the divisions in separate places. In time, each division will grow into a new clump. Plants that spread by runners can also be divided.

In layering, a gardener bends a branch of a plant down to the ground and partly covers it with soil. Roots grow from the buried stem, and shoots grow up. When the new plant has a good root system, it can be cut away from the parent plant. This method is used for roses, as well as blackberry and raspberry bushes.

IRELAND'S POTATO FAMINE

When a plant has desirable traits, it makes sense to grow more of those plants by vegetative propagation. That way, growers can be sure the new plants will have the traits they want. But it's important for plants to have genetic variety, too. In Ireland, a disaster taught people that lesson.

Relying on one potato variety led to a disaster in Ireland. Today farmers grow many varieties.

In the early 1800's, potatoes were Ireland's biggest crop. In fact, 90 percent of the people depended on potatoes. Most of them grew one variety, called the lumper, because it produced high yields. Lumpers were planted each year from cut-up seed potatoes—tubers saved from the previous year.

But, in 1845, a fungal disease called late blight hit the potato crop. Lumpers were very susceptible. The blight killed 40 percent of the crop that year and wiped out almost the entire crop in 1846. People began to starve, and thousands left Ireland for Britain or America. By the time the famine ended in 1851, some 1.5 million people had died. Another 1 million had emigrated.

About 25 varieties of potatoes are grown in Ireland today. They include types with high resistance to blight. And they don't include lumpers.

A cutting is just what it sounds like—a piece of stem or a leaf cut from a plant. Many cuttings grow roots if their ends are put in water or damp soil. Some plants, including African violets, will grow from leaf cuttings. Other plants grow better from stem cuttings. Plant growers often dust the end of a cutting with a chemical called rooting hormone, which encourages roots to form.

In grafting, a shoot or branch from one plant is inserted into the stem of another plant. If the graft takes, the shoot or branch grows as if it had always been part of the other plant. Grafting is often used with apple trees and roses as a way to combine traits of different plants. A branch of an apple tree that produces flavorful apples might be grafted onto the trunk of an apple tree with extra-hardy roots, for example.

A peperomia grows roots from a stem cutting.

23

By using these methods, growers can produce lots of plants that have identical traits. This is important when the grower wants plants with specific features, such as flowers of a certain color. And for the most part these methods take less effort, and cost less, than growing plants from seed. Some crops are grown entirely by vegetative propagation. For example, sugarcane is traditionally grown from "seed cane," cuttings of sugarcane stalk that are planted horizontally in the ground. One cane stalk can produce about twenty new sugarcane plants.

Scientists have also developed new ways to clone plants. In the lab, they grow small bits of plant tissue in special mixtures of chemicals. This is called tissue culture. Using tissue culture, a single sugarcane stalk can produce about two thousand healthy seedlings—an army of green clones!

Different plants, such as this plum and crab apple, can be combined through grafting.

IM-PLANTS

Tissue culture is being paired with another new technology —genetic engineering—to produce improved varieties of plants. In genetic engineering, scientists transfer a gene from one living thing to another by implanting it. In this way, they can give plants traits that they do not normally have. Once they've added a new trait this way, scientists can use tissue culture and other kinds of vegetative propagation to produce lots of plants that carry the trait.

This new technology can be used to produce plants that resist disease and have lots of other desirable traits. For example, some soil bacteria make a chemical, Bt, that kills insects. Scientists have taken the gene that causes the bacteria to make Bt and placed it in corn. They've created a new type of corn that resists insect pests. Farmers don't need to spray this corn with insecticides—it makes its own Bt.

Genetic engineering holds promise for producing crops to feed the world's growing population. But this technology has sparked a lot of debate. Many people worry that by tinkering with the genes inside plants, people may upset the balance of nature.

High-tech corn resists insect pests.

2

Growing Plants Without Seeds

It's easy to grow plants using their natural ability to reproduce without seeds. It's rewarding, too—plants grow quickly this way. In this section, you'll find out how to grow several kinds of plants from plant parts such as tubers, stems, and leaves. Your plants will grow well if you give them what they need: sunlight, moisture, and good soil.

Potato Patch

Plant a potato patch outside in spring. By the end of summer, you'll harvest a potato crop. Here's what to do:

Buy some potatoes and place them in a warm place, such as a room in your house. When their tiny eyes get bigger and start to sprout, it's time to plant.

You can plant whole potatoes or ask an adult to cut the potatoes into pieces for planting. Each piece should have at least one eye. The eyes will produce the shoots and roots of the new plants.

Right: Seed potatoes are cut up for planting. Each section should have an eye.

Below: The eyes of this potato have begun to sprout.

Plant potatoes in good soil, in a trench about 6 to 8 inches deep.

28

Dig a trench in your garden about 6 to 8 inches deep. Place the potatoes in the trench with most of the eyes pointing upward. Space them about 12 inches apart, and cover them with soil. Use a watering can to moisten the soil. Keep the plants well watered all summer long.

As the new plants begin growing, mound more soil around their stems. Keep adding soil around the stems as they grow. Tubers will grow in the soil around the stems, so adding more soil will help more tubers to form.

In early to mid summer the plants will bloom. A few weeks after you see flowers, gently dig into the soil on one side of the plants. You should find tiny potatoes growing. Some may be big enough to pick and eat as "new" potatoes. Put soil back over the rest and let them continue to grow.

Late in the summer, as the plants start to die back, dig all the potatoes out of the ground. You can eat them right away or store them for up to nine months. If you want to store them, let them air-dry for a week or two. Then put them in a cool, dark place so they won't sprout.

Right above: Tubers grow in the soil around a potato plant stem.

Right below: Harvest the potatoes by digging up the plants in late summer or fall.

The African violet is one of many houseplants that can be grown from cuttings.

Plants from Cuttings

Gardeners and commercial growers use leaf and stem cuttings to grow new plants quickly. Leaf cuttings work well with plants such as African violets, peperomias, jade plants, and begonias. Here's how to do it:

Take a leaf, with its stem attached, from your plant.

Stand the leaf upright with its stem partly buried in moist sterile planting mixture. You can also use sand, vermiculite, potting soil, or peat moss.

Cover the planted leaf with a glass jar to keep it moist and healthy. A tiny new plant will grow where the stem hits the moist potting mixture.

Stem cuttings work well with Swedish ivy and many other houseplants.

Using scissors, cut a 3- to 6-inch piece of a stem from your plant. The tip of the stem usually gives the fastest results. Be sure the section includes some leaves. Cut off the lowest leaves so that the lower part of the stem is bare, but keep at least four leaves at the top.

Place the bare end of the stem in a small container of water, keeping the leaves out of the water. Place the container in medium light but not direct sunlight. Add water as needed to keep the level the same.

Roots will begin to grow in the water. When the roots are an inch or more long, you can move the new plant to a flower pot. Plant it in potting soil.

Above: New African violet plants will grow from the base of these leaves.

Right: The lower leaves were removed from this peperomia stem before it was placed in water.

31

Multiply by Division

Division is a fast way to multiply plants such as hostas and spider plants that have lots of short stems growing out of the ground or at the base of the plant.

Dig up the plant, or tip it out of its pot. Pull away the stems growing around the outside of the clump, keeping any roots attached. If the stems are too tightly bound together, ask an adult to help you cut the clump apart.

Plant stems with well-developed roots and leaves in new pots (or new places in the garden). Stems with few or no roots can be rooted as cuttings.

Left: New plants are starting to grow from the base of this house plant.

Above: The new plants can be separated from the parent and grown in their own pots.

32

Graft a Coleus

The leaves of coleus plants have bold patterns and colors. You can create a coleus with two different leaf colors by grafting. This technique is challenging, but worth trying.

Buy two coleus plants with different colored leaves. Ask an adult to cut the center stem of each plant with a sharp knife. Cut the stems of both plants the same way, so that they'll fit together.

Working quickly so that the cuts will not dry out, fit the top of one plant onto the base of the other. Put a little petroleum jelly around the joint to seal it. Then tape the joint together with masking tape. (If you use too much petroleum jelly, the tape won't stick. Wipe some off and try again.) Spread more petroleum jelly over the taped area to make sure moisture will not escape.

After several weeks, if the plants look healthy, you can remove the tape. Now you have a plant with leaves of two colors. You can try this with tomato or potato plants, too.

Above: A stick and clothespins make a "splint" to hold grafted stems.

Below: After the graft takes, red leaves grow from a green coleus.

33

3

Investigating Plant Clones

What do plants need to make clones? How do light, moisture, and other conditions affect the process? In this chapter you'll find some activities and experiments that will help you answer these and other questions. Many of the activities use houseplants that can be purchased anytime, so they can be done year-round. Others are best done in the garden, during warm weather.

Do Cuttings Grow Better with a Rooting Hormone?

Growers often use products called rooting hormones to help their cuttings grow. Do these powders, gels, and liquids really make a difference? Decide what you think, and then do this experiment to see if you are right. You can get rooting hormone at a garden center or through mail-order supply houses like those listed on page 46.

What you need
* African violet leaf cuttings, or cuttings from another houseplant
* Rooting hormone
* Planting mixture (sterile potting soil, sand, vermiculite, or peat moss)
* Plant containers

What to Do:

1. Use scissors to take several stem or leaf cuttings from your plant. Dip the cut ends in rooting hormone, and then set them upright in containers filled with planting mixture. Push the stem ends down into the growing medium.

2. Take several other cuttings. Do not dip the ends, but put them in plant mixture as above.

3. Label the cuttings so you'll remember which is which. Place the containers in medium light, and keep the planting mix evenly moist.

Results: In a few weeks, new plants will begin to grow. Note which containers have new plants first, and compare the growth rates of the plants as they grow.

Conclusions: What do your results show about the use of hormones on cuttings?

35

What you need

* Potatoes
* A sunny garden spot
* Shovel and watering can
* Plant markers

Big Eyes or Small Eyes: Which Potatoes Grow Faster?

Do potatoes with tiny eyes grow faster than potatoes with large eyes once both are planted in soil? Or doesn't eye size matter? Based on what you know about tubers, decide what you think. Then do this experiment to test your answer.

What to Do:

1. Keep several potatoes in a warm place until their eyes swell and begin to sprout. Then buy several other potatoes of the same type, but with small eyes.

2. Plant several of each kind in your garden. (See "Potato Patch" on page 27 for planting and growing directions.) Label the potatoes so you remember which had the small eyes and which had the big eyes. Cover them with a similar amount of soil.

3. Check your potato patch every day. When plants poke through the soil, keep a journal of their growth.

Results: Note which plants grow first, and which grow biggest as they mature.

Conclusion: What do your results tell you about the relationship of eye size to plant growth?

Do Leaf Cuttings Grow Better Undercover?

African violets, begonias, and some other plants have the amazing ability to produce new little plants from leaf cutting. Will these clones grow best in the open air or under the shelter of a glass, which will trap moisture? Make a guess, based on what you know about the way plants grow. Then check your answer with this experiment.

What you need
* African violet, pepperomia, begonia, or jade plant
* Planting mixture (sterile potting soil, sand, vermiculite, and peat moss
* Plant containers
* Drinking glass or other clear cover

What to Do:

1. Moisten some planting mix with water, and put an equal amount of the damp mix in each container.
2. Cut some individual leaves at the point where they join the plant stem. Include the short leaf stems, or petioles, with the leaves.

3. Stand the leaves upright in the containers, pushing the stems ½ to 1 inch into the planting mix.

4. Keep some leaves uncovered. Cover others with a glass or other clear cover.

5. Place the containers in medium light. Keep the planting mix evenly moist.

6. In a few weeks, check for roots by gently pulling the leaves. If they resist, roots are forming. If they have no roots, replant them. After roots form, new plantlets will grow.

Results: Which leaf cuttings produce roots and plantlets first?

Conclusion: If some leaf cuttings grew better than others, what made the difference? What do your results tell you about the conditions leaf cuttings need? Make up your own experiments to see how other conditions, such as temperature and light, affect growth.

How Much Food Does a Potato Sprout Need?

The eyes of a potato tuber give rise to new sprouts. The flesh of the tuber provides food for the sprout until it can develop a good root system. Will the amount of potato food around the eye affect how fast the new plant will grow? Think about your answer. Then do this experiment to find out.

What you need
* Potatoes
* A sunny garden spot
* Shovel and watering can
* Plant markers

What to Do:

1. Keep the potatoes in a warm place until they produce sprouts an inch or so in length. Then select several potatoes that have sprouts that are about the same size.
2. Ask an adult to help cut up the potatoes. Cut some pieces with just a little flesh around each eye. Cut others with more flesh around each eye. Leave one potato whole. Remove extra eyes, so that each potato piece has one eye.
3. Plant the potatoes in your garden. (See "Potato Patch" on page 27 for instructions.) Label the plantings, so you'll remember which is which.
4. Keep the potato patch watered, and check the plants daily.

Results: Which plants grow fastest?

Conclusion: What do your results tell you about the amount of food new potato plants need?

More Activities With Plant Clones

1. Check out an onion bulb. Have an adult cut through the center of an onion from tip to base so you can see the bud inside. To grow an onion plant, set an onion bulb in a container of water so that only the base stays wet. New roots will grow from the base, and bud inside will grow into a stem. When your onion tops are about 4 inches high, ask an adult to cut down through the middle of the bulb to see the leaves forming there.

An onion cut in half.

Six new strawberry plants, each in its own pot, have grown from the parent plant.

42

2. Raise a family of strawberry plants. Start with one plant in a pot. Keep it watered and in full sun. Before long, it will send out runners. Put the tip of each runner in a new pot with potting soil. You can use a stone to hold the runner down while a new plant grows. See how many new plants you can grow from the parent plant.

3. Have your carrot and eat it, too. A carrot is a root that stores food for the carrot plant, and you can grow a new plant from the top of the root. First, take off any wilted leaves at the top of the carrot. Then have an adult cut off the top 2 inches. You can eat the rest, but save that top end. Put it cut end down in a bowl of water, with pebbles to hold it upright. New leaves will grow from the top. You can do this with beets, turnips, and parsnips, too.

Right above: Carrot and beet tops set up to grow new roots.

Right below: New leaves sprout from a beet top.

43

Results and Conclusions

Here are some possible results and conclusions for the activities on pages 35 to 40. Because many conditions affect the way plants grow, you may not get the same results. If your outcomes differ, try to think of reasons why. What do you think led to your results? Repeat the activities, and see if the outcomes are the same.

Do cuttings grow better with a rooting hormone?
The chemicals in rooting hormone stimulate the roots to grow faster. More roots should help the new plant grow better.

Big eyes or small eyes: Which potatoes grow faster?
The big eyes will probably grow faster. They have already started to sprout, so they have a head start on the small eyes.

Do leaf cuttings grow better undercover?
Your results will depend on many factors, including the type of plant you use. Plants that are sensitive to drying out may grow better under a cover that traps moisture. But other plants don't like too much moisture. If you succeed in keeping the containers equally moist, the cuttings may grow equally well.

How much food does a potato sprout need?
A sprout doesn't need much food to get started, so the amount of potato around the eyes should not affect growth. Seed potatoes are usually cut into small pieces for planting to get the most new plants from each potato.

Some Words About Plant Clones

asexual reproduction Reproduction involving only one sex. A new plant that grows in this way has only one parent.

bulbs Squat underground stems with thick fleshy leaves that store food. Bulblets grow at the sides of the bulb, producing new plants.

clone A group of asexually produced, genetically identical individuals; also, a member of the group.

corms Squat underground stems that store food and can produce new plants.

genes Materials inside cells that determine the traits of living things.

nodes Points on a stem from which new stems, leaves, or roots can grow.

pollen A powdery substance that contains the male sex cells of a flower.

rhizomes Stems that grow horizontally below the soil.

runners Horizontal stems that grow out from the plant along the soil.

sexual reproduction Reproduction that involves two sexes, male and female.

tubers Swollen tips of rhizomes that can produce new plant shoots.

vegetative propagation The methods people use to grow plants without seeds.

vegetative reproduction The process by which plants produce offspring asexually.

45

Sources for Rooting Hormone

Connecticut Valley Biological Supply
82 Valley Road, P.O. Box 326
Southampton, MA 01073
(800) 628-7748
www.ctvalleybio.com

Gardener's Supply Company
128 Intervale Road
Burlington, VT 05401
(888) 833-1412
www.gardeners.com

For More Information

Books

Baker, Wendy. *Plants.* Two-Can, 2000.

Bradley, Clare. *Fun With Gardening: 50 Great Projects Kids Can Plant Themselves.* Southwater, 2000.

Handelsman, Judith F. *Gardens from Garbage: How to Grow Indoor Plants from Recycled Kitchen Scraps.* Millbrook Press, 1994.

Hershey, David R. *Plant Biology Science Projects.* John Wiley & Sons, 1995.

Spilsbury, Louise and Richard. *Plant Reproduction.* Heinemann Library, 2003.

Vancleave, Janice Pratt. *Janice Vancleave's Plants: Mind-Boggling Experiments You Can Turn into Science Fair Projects.* Bt Bound, 1999.

Websites

American Horticultural Society
Find all kinds of plant-related information at this site.
http://www.ahs.org/youth_gardening/kids_grow.htm

Gardening for Kids
This site has plant-growing tips for young gardeners.
http://www.geocities.com/EnchantedForest/Glade/3313/

Index